ANALYTICAL DIAGRAMS FOR I.T. SYSTEMS

ISBN: 978-1-326-05786-2

Copyright © 2014 Andreas Sofroniou.

Copyright © 2014 Andreas Sofroniou.

ANALYTICAL DIAGRAMS FOR I.T. SYSTEMS

ISBN: 978-1-326-05786-2

DEDICATED

TO ALL THE INTERNATIONAL ORGANISATIONS AND GOVERNMENT DEPARTMENTS, WHOSE PROBLEMS WITH SYSTEMS, PEOPLE AND BUSINESS GAVE ME, AS A CONSULTANT, THE AFFLUENCE I DESERVED.

FOR THAT I THANK THEE,

Andreas

CONTENTS   PAGE

PREFACE

As an author and a long serving Systems Consultant, I am excited about the draft diagrammatical techniques described in this book. They are proving their worth in a troublesome area of systematic data processing: the analysis and definition of what a new or a converted system should do if it is to be of most value to the people who are paying for it.

The discipline consists of an evolving set of tools and techniques which have grown out of the success of structured analysis and the use of diagrams. The underlined concept is the building of a logical (non-physical) model of a system, using graphical techniques which enable users to get a clear picture of the system-to-be and how its parts will fit together to meet the users requirements.

The overall methodology is based on the principles of building a system top-down by successive refinement; first producing a hand drawn data flow, then developing detailed data flows in draft modes, until the users agree that the modelling will very closely represent their needs, as their original requirements were listed.

Further on, it is recognised that good development involves iteration; one has to be prepared to refine the logical model and the physical design in the light of information resulting from the use of an early version of that model or design.

In writing this book, the author distinguishes the work of analysis (defining what the system 'will' do) from the work of design (defining 'how' it will do it); recognising that analysts often design and designers often do analysis.

The author's idea of using draft hand drawn diagrams during the initial design of every stage of the system development is what is actually included in this book. All the examples of the diagrams shown are hand written. The system and its hand written diagrams are based on a system developed by the author for a large company.

Finally, the book includes the issues that arise in changing over to the recommended techniques, instead of the traditional approaches, with their implications for management control of projects, and the benefit that one can expect.

1. DEVELOPMENTAL DIFFICULTIES

1.1 Systems Analysis

In many ways systems analysis is the toughest part of the development of a system. It may not be the technical difficulties of the work involved though many projects demand that the analysts have deep knowledge of the current operating systems technology. There will be political issues that arise, especially in larger projects where the new system will serve several, possibly conflicting, interest groups.

Added all the problems are the communicating difficulties that arise in any situation where people of different backgrounds, and different vocabularies, with different views of the world have to work together. It is the compounding of these difficulties together that makes systems analysis so hard and demanding; the fact that the analyst must play the middle man between the user communities, who have a gut feeling for their problems.

The analyst must make a match between what is currently possible and available in our onrushing information technology and what is worth doing for the business, as run by the people in it.

Making the match in a way which is acceptable to all parties and will stand the test of time is the hardest part of the effort. If it is done well, then no matter how difficult the design and programming, the system which is built will serve the needs of the business.

If it is done poorly, then no matter how excellent the implementation, the system will not be what the organisation and the users require. In such cases, the costs and frustration will outweigh the benefits.

In making that match we need all the help we can get. It is, therefore, of utmost importance that we deal with the users requirements sensibly and adhere to their functioning problems wisely.

In order to make communications easier a good analyst will draft the diagram by hand so that he/she, without any unnecessary delay, obtain the agreement to go ahead with the formalising of the diagrams and the narrative by using the computer-aided case tools. A formal discussion will then follow for the signing off of this stage of development.

1. 2 Blaming Tools

Even with the best possible analytical tools, some of the problems will always be with us. For instance, no analytical tool will enable analysts to know what is in a user's mind without being told. Nonetheless, it is the theme of this book that the problems of analysis can be significantly eased with the logical tools.

There is no way of showing a vivid tangible model of the system to users. Further on, it is hard for users to imagine what the new system is going to do for them until it is actually in operation, by which time it is usually too late.

The distinguished cry of many users is: "What do I know what I want till I see what I get?" The pictorial, the hand drawn diagrammatical representations, in this 'book give the users a better 'model' of the system than it was possible until now.

English narrative is too vague and long-winded and old fashioned flowcharts do more harm than good. There is no systematic way of recording user preferences and trade-offs, especially in terms of immediate access to data. The analyst has to draw out the users preferences for various aspects of the new system.

In such cases, the functional specifications matter. The analyst can use the tools of structured systems analysis described in this book to prepare a functional specification that:

1.   Is well-understood and fully agreed by the users,

2.   Sets out the logical requirements of the system without dictating a physical implementation,

3.   Expresses preferences and trade-offs.

The building of a logical model clearly communicates to users what the systems will do and what it will not do. This is essentially and crucially an important exercise in terms of the cost of fixing costs later on.

Making changes on pieces of paper is cheap; making changes in code is several times more expensive. It certainly cannot be afforded to wait for users to see what they get, before they know what they want.

9

1.3 Tools Fitting Together

Before examining each of the tools of structured analysis, an overview of each tool will show their relationship to one another; by seeing how they can be used in relatively simple analysis situation.

The organisation referred to in this book is a book selling establishment; receiving orders, ordering stock from the appropriate publishers, production of invoices and other parts of the way the company deals with orders.

A systems analyst has been assigned, with the responsibility of investigating and specifying the required new system.

1.4 Draw a logical data flow diagram

At the most general level, just like the present system, the new system will take book orders, check them against a file of books available, check against some file to see that the customer's credit is okay, and cause the book/s ordered to be sent out with an invoice.

This activity can be shown in a logical data flow diagram (DFD) thus:

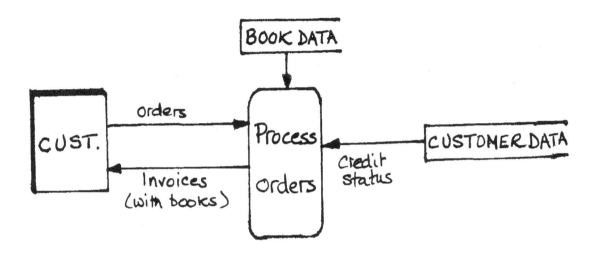

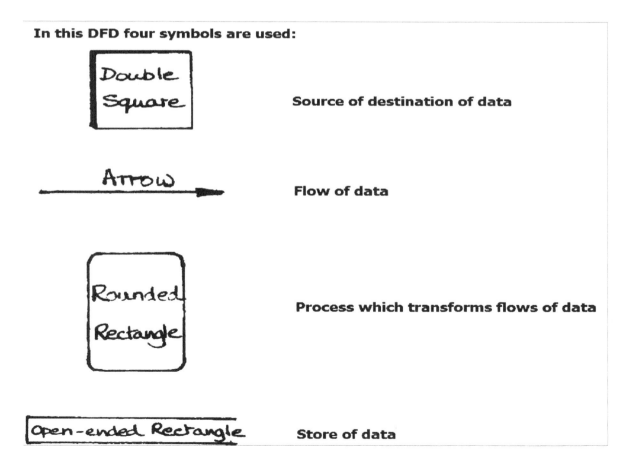

In this DFD four symbols are used:

Double Square — **Source of destination of data**

Arrow — **Flow of data**

Rounded Rectangle — **Process which transforms flows of data**

Open-ended Rectangle — **Store of data**

These symbols and the concepts they stand for are at the logical level; a flow of data may physically be contained on line, in a letter, or invoice, telephone call, program to program, via the internet, satellite data link, anywhere data pass from one entity or process to another.

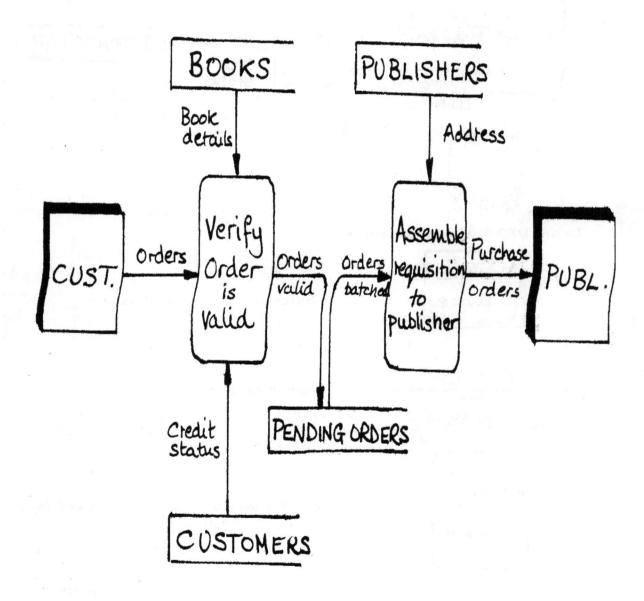

The reader will see from the previous DFD that, as each order is checked, it is put in a data store of pending orders, until a batch of orders can be assembled into a bulk order.

In the following DFD the reader will notice that each publisher will send a shipping notice with each shipment, detailing its contents, which in turn is compared with the order that was placed to ensure that the right numbers of the correct titles have been sent.

In this case, there must be another data store, named 'Publisher Orders' which can be interrogated. Once the right books become available, the orders to the individual customers are sent.

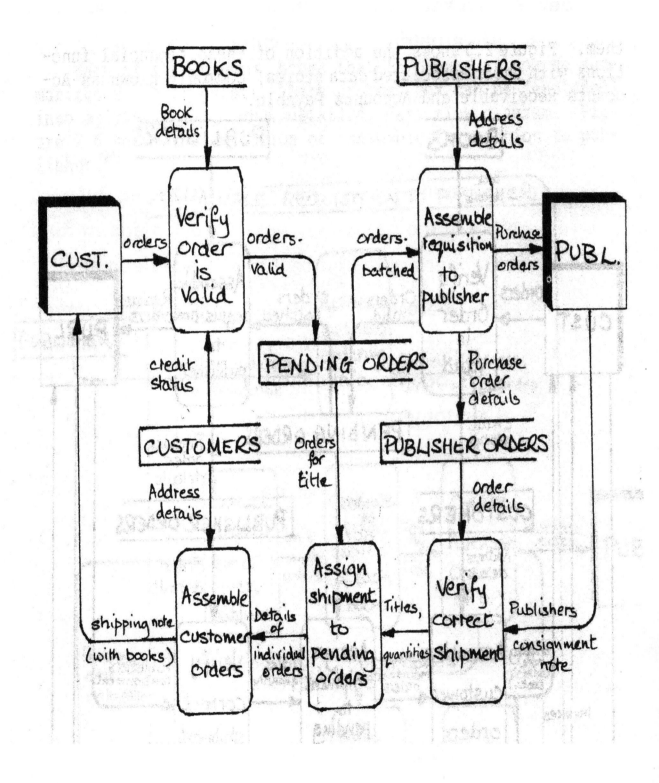

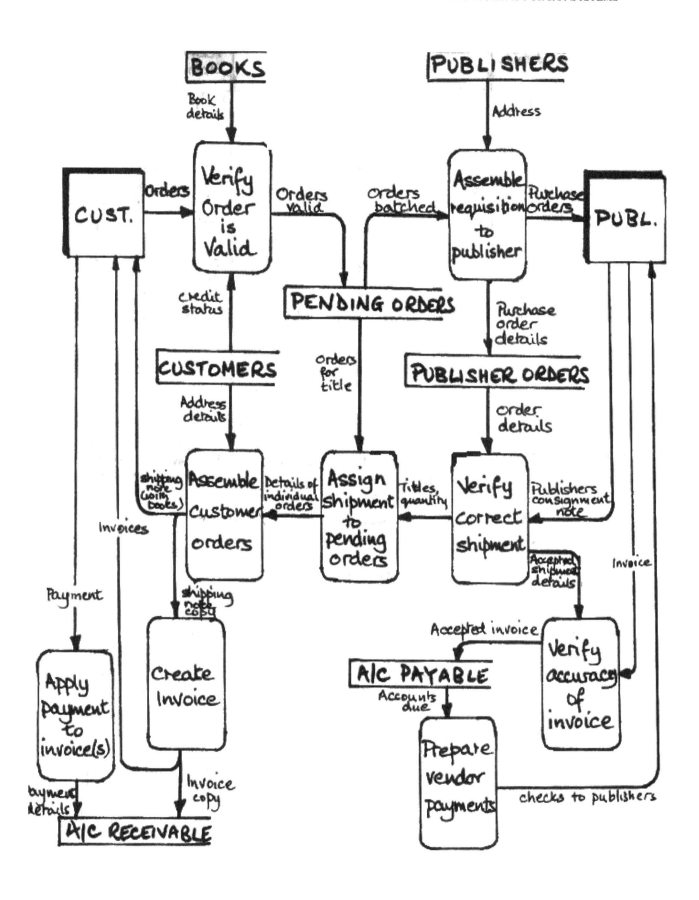

For the sake of clarity, the logical functions for the creation and the maintenance of the customer file, the book file and the publisher file have not been shown, nor are the handling of any enquiries.

These functions will be dealt with in the next chapter.

Each of the process boxes that are shown summarises a lot of detail. Each process, therefore, can be exploded into a lower level, more detailed data flow diagram.

If necessary, each component process box can be broken down to a third level of detail.

In the next chapter, guidelines with details for drawing and handling explosions will be explained further.

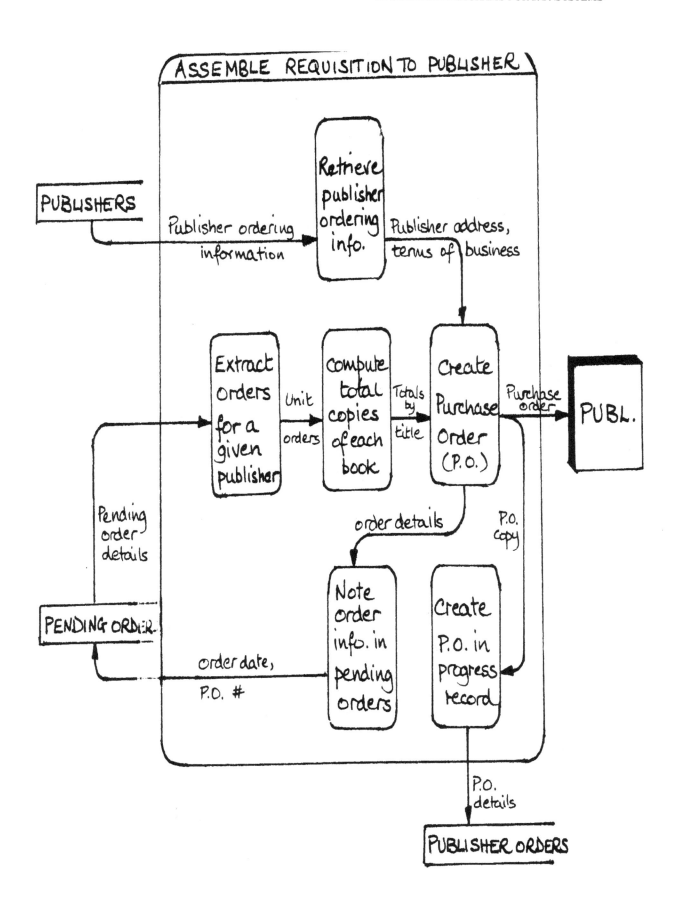

A very important point regarding large scale DFDs, is that since it is a logical data flow diagram, it is easy to envisage several physical implementations.

As we now have a 'map of the forest', we can read off several different alternative solutions by drawing the system boundary around different processes and data stores.

The following diagram shows two such possibilities.

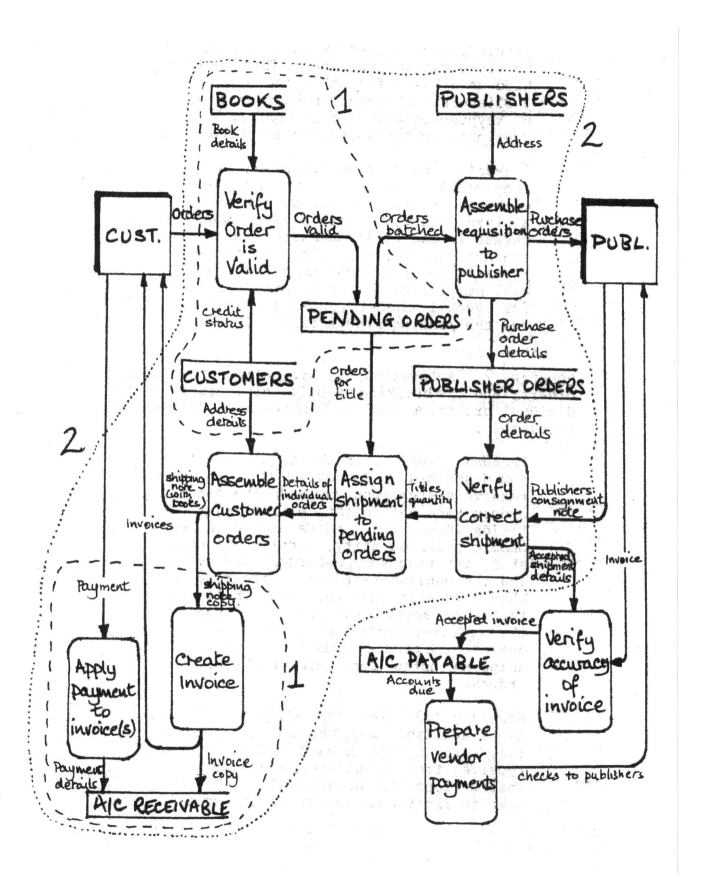

Boundary 1:

Automating order validation, as well as invoicing and accounts receivable, while leaving the batching of orders all purchasing functions to be done manually.

Boundary 2:

Automating the production of purchase orders, and the breaking of bulk shipments into individual orders, as well as order entry and accounts receivable.

1.4 Putting the detail in a data dictionary

In the data flow diagrams of the previous section, names were given to the data flows, data stores and processes, which are as descriptive and meaningful as possible, being short enough to fit the on the diagram.

As soon as the analyst and the users start looking more closely, for instance, to answer what exactly is meant by 'orders', the team members find themselves getting quickly into great detail, perhaps specifying the layout of the order form, gathering samples, and so on.

At this stage the project stays at the logical level, identifying each of the data elements that are present in a data flow, giving them meaningful names, defining each one, and organising them so that one can easily look up the definition.

This is where the meaning of orders will be dealt with. At the very least an order for a book will carry some identification of the order, the customer's name and address, and the details of at least one book.

These will be shown the following breakdown:

```
ORDER
    ORDER-IDENTIFICATION
    CUSTOMER-DETAILS
    BOOK-DETAILS
```

and we can expand these further. with notes:

```
ORDER
    ORDER-IDENTIFICATION
        ORDER-DATE
        CUSTOMER-ORDER-NUM.......usually present
    CUSTOMER-DETAILS
        ORGANIZATION-NAME
        PERSON-AUTHORIZING.......optional
            FIRST-NAME...........may be initial only
            LAST-NAME
        PHONE
            AREA-CODE
            EXCHANGE
            NUMBER
            EXTENSION...........optional
        SHIP-TO-ADDRESS
            STREET
            CITY-COUNTY
            STATE-ZIP
        BILL-TO-ADDRESS.........If not present, same as
            STREET                 SHIP-TO-ADDRESS
            CITY-COUNTY
            STATE-ZIP
    BOOK-DETAILS.................One or more iterations of this
                                   group of data elements
        AUTHOR-NAME.............One or more iterations of this
        TITLE                      data element

        ISBN....................International Standard Book
                                   Number, (optional)
        LOCN....................Library of Congress Number,
                                   (optional)
        PUBLISHER-NAME..........Optional
```

Note that this data structure for an order tells us nothing about form layout, field size, etc. while it omits this physical detail, it is precise enough for the analyst and the user to review for errors and omissions.

For instance, the user might well say, "If the BILL-TO-ADDRESS is given, we need to record the name of the person to whose attention the invoice is sent", and then the analyst can add in another data element.

Each of the data elements referred to in the data structure of ORDER may need to be defined separately.

For instance, what do we mean by ISBN, the International Standard Book Number? It is necessary to be able to quickly locate an explanation that the ISBN is thirteen digit number, divided into five groups.

For example: ISBN: 978-1-84753-147-6.

This is the ISBN for the book published by Lulu.com, in the U.S.A., by Andreas Sofroniou, under the title of

23

'Management of I.T., Changes, Risks, Workshops, Epistemology'.

The technique for documenting data element definitions is explained later on in this book.

For the moment, if we had a definition and explanation of each data flow, the contents of each data store, and of each data element of which they were composed, and if we could arrange those definitions in alphabetical order for easy reference, we would have a data dictionary for the system.

The techniques, implementations, and advantages of data dictionaries are discussed at length later on in this book.

The most important benefit for the analysts is that they can describe data flows and data stores by giving a single meaningful name, knowing that all the details for which that name stands are readily available whenever required.

2. DEFINING THE LOGIC OF THE PROCESSES

2.1 Data Elements

With each data element in the system defined, we can begin to explore what is going on in the processes. For example, what is meant to 'Apply Payment to Invoice'? We have seen that each process can be exploded into lower level processes.

Suppose one such lower level process, 'Verify Discount', involve checking that the correct discount has been applied. If the analyst inquires, 'What is the Discount Policy'? He may well be shown a memo or a page in procedures manual, explaining something like:

'Trade discount to established booksellers is 20%. For private customers and libraries, 5% discount is allowed on orders for 6 books or more, 10% on orders for 20 books or more, and 15% on orders for 50 or more. Trade orders for 20 books and over receive the 10% discount in addition to the trade discount'.

This is a very simple piece of what is called 'external logic'; external in the sense that it concerns itself with business policy, procedures or clerical rules, as opposed to 'internal logic', which specifies the way in which the computer will implement them.

Simple though this example may be, policy logic can very quickly; get confusing, especially since exceptions and policy changes get dealt with by writing more memos, rather than re-writing the original policy document.

The analyst needs tools to picture the structure of the logic and express policies in a comprehensive unambiguous form.

First of these tools is the 'decision tree', as shown in the next figure. The branches of the tree correspond to each of the logical possibilities; the way in which the amount of the discount depends on the combination of possibilities is self-evident.

As a tool for sketching out logical structure and for getting the user to confirm that the policy logic expressed is correct, the decision tree is excellent. It is possible to read off the combination of circumstances that leads to each action directly and clearly.

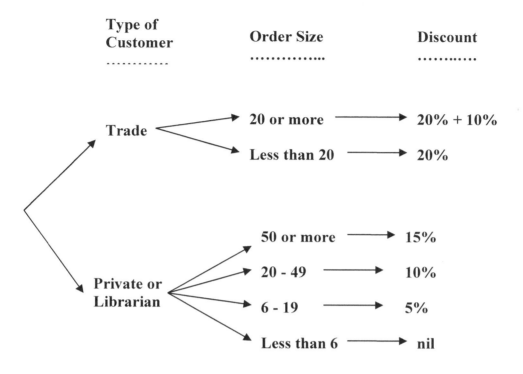

While the decision tree shows the 'bare bones' of the decision structure very clearly, it does not lend itself easily to the incorporation of instructions or calculations,

If we need to write down the logic as a step-by-step set of instructions, including the decision structure and intermediate calculations or actions we may prefer to use a strict form of English as shown on the next figure.

This form of English has bee called Structured English, because it uses logical constructs similar to those of Structured Programming. Instructions to carry out actions which involve no decision are written out as imperative sentences.

Where a decision must be made, it is expressed as a combination of IF, THEN, ELSE SO, with IF and ELSE aligned appropriately to show the structure of the decision.

DISCOUNT POLICY

Add up the total number of volumes on the order (in the quantity column)

> IF the order is from a trade customer
> and-IF   the order calls 20 or more volumes
> THEN discount is 30%
> ELSE (order is for less than 20)
> SO: DISCOUNT IS 20%

> ELSE (order is from a private customer or librarian)

> So-IF   the order calls for 50 or more volumes
> discount is 15%
> ELSE IF the order is for 20 to 49 volumes
> discount is 10%
> ELSE IF the order is for 6 to 19 volumes
> discount is 5%
> ELSE IF (order is for less than 6 volumes)
> SO: no discount is given

We can make the Structured English (and the decision tree) more precise and compact by using, where relevant, terms which are defined in the data dictionary. For instance, we could define ORDER-SIZE as a data element which can take up four values:

> SMALL   - 5 or fewer volumes
> MEDIUM - 6 to 19 volumes
> LARGE   - 20 to 49 volumes
> BULK   - 50 or more

The first part would then read

> IF the order is from a trade customer
> And-IF ORDER-SIZE is LARGE or BULK
> THEN: discount is 30%

2.2 Data Stores: Contents

As we build up the data flow diagrams, we identified places where data was held from one transaction to the next, or stored permanently because it described some aspect of the world outside the system.

The analyst must obviously specify the data elements that are held in each data store, in a similar way to the specification of each data flow.

Since data can only get into a data store via some data flow, and cannot get out unless it has been put in, the contents of a data store can be read off from the specification of the incoming and outgoing data flows.

The logical contents of each data store are held in the data dictionary under the name of the data store. Just as with a data flow, the individual data elements in the data store are defined elsewhere in the data dictionary.

For example, a data store called 'BOOKS', which is used in order verification entering with a title or an author and retrieving book details. What do we mean by 'book details'?

If we look up BOOK-DETAILS in the data dictionary, we will find the following:

```
BOOK-DETAILS
     AUTHOR-NAME........One or more iterations
     ORGANIZATION-AFFILIATION.....University, corporation
     TITLE
     ISBN.................International Standard Book
                                Number, (optional)
     LOCN.................Library of Congress Number,
                                (optional)
     PUBLISHER-NAME......Optional, see file of abbrev-
                                iations
     PRICE-HARDBACK
     PRICE-PAPER
     PUBLICATION-DATE....May be iterations if editions
```

Clearly, as all these data elements are present in the data flow, they must be present in the data store.

2.3 Immediate Access

Much harder and yet more critical than the task of specifying contents, is the task of deciding hat immediate accesses to each data store are needed by the user.

31

For example, let us suppose we have decided to have the BOOKs file available on-line. The data element which uniquely identifies each book is the IISBN. But if we make that the primary key of the file, and have immediate access only by that key, it means that we have to know the ISBN of a book in order to display its title, subject-code, publisher, price, etc.

This is comparable to having to know a person's insurance policy number in order find their policy, or having to know the part-number of a part in order to know the price.

We much more frequently want immediate access based on the name of something, and this means that the analyst must specify multiple accesses to the file.

In this case, the user might quite rightly decide to display book details on his screen as a result of keying in either the name of an author (in which case he might get several books), or a subject heading (in which case he would almost certainly get several screens full), or the actual title, or the ISBN.

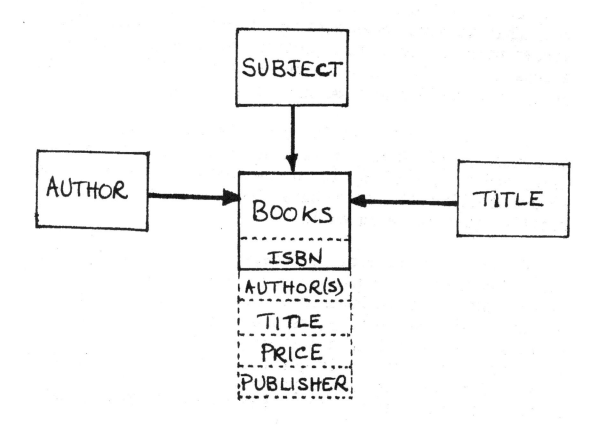

This diagram indicates that a file exists describing books with an ISBN as the primary key, and additional data elements describing attributes of each book, such as author, price, etc.

The fact that ISBN is shown as being the primary key (within the solid rectangle) implies that, 'Given an ISBN, show me the author/s and title', can be answered immediately.

A query such as, 'Given a publisher, show me all their titles', cannot be answered immediately with the accesses defined as shown in the diagram. However, the publisher does appear in each BOOK record, so it is possible to sort the file on the publisher field, or to write a program which reads the entire file, extracting book records for any given publisher.

It is true that part of the ISBN is a publisher code, but the enquirer my not always know the code.

On the other hand, the details on AUTHOR, BOOKS, and TITLES can be answered immediately. The SUBJECT access is not an attribute of BOOKS. As an index it can be included in the immediate access diagram, thus telling the data base designer that this facility must be designed in.

The immediate access diagram can be used to record the information that we need about user preferences and the value of each access in the business.

2.4 Functional Specification

The logical data flow diagram shows the sources and destinations of data, and so by implication the boundaries of the system, identifies and names the groups of data elements that connect one function to another and the data stores which they access.

Each data flow is analysed, its structures and the definitions of its component data elements stored in the data dictionary.

When the complete package is prepared for a new system, we have a logical functional specification, a detailed statement of what the system is to do, which is as free as possible from physical considerations of how it will implemented.

This type of functional specification gives the designer a clear idea of the end results of what he has to achieve, and written evidence of the users' preferences.

Often, as already indicated, the analyst and designer will go through several iterations of setting up trial physical designs, working out their technical and cost implications, changing some features, and trying again.

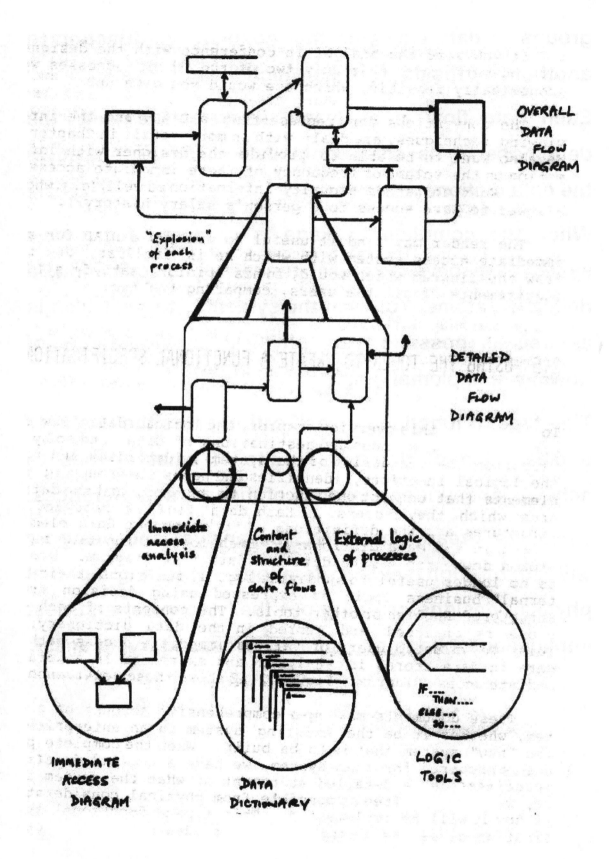

3. DRAWING DATAFLOW DIAGRAMS

In analysis we need to recognise external entities and datastores, as well as dataflows and transforms, or processes. In order to represent our logical system fully, we need to add symbols to the simple program graph. Also, since we need to describe our processes clearly, we adopt a rectangle with rounded corners as the process symbol.

3.1 Examining Symbol Conventions

[Note to the reader: all eleven pages that follow have been scanned from a real system analysis and subsequently used for training analysts, designers and users.]

External Entity

Please see the diagrammatical representation as shown on the next page.

EXTERNAL ENTITY

External entities are most usually logical classes of things or people which represent a source or destination of transactions, e.g., Customers, Employees, Aircraft, Tactical Units, Suppliers, Taxpayers, Policy-holders.   They may also be a specific source or destination, e.g., Accounts Department, IRS, Office of the President, Warehouse. Where the system we are considering accepts data from another system or provides data to it, that other system is an external entity.

An external entity can be symbolized by a "solid" square, with the upper and left sides in double thickness to make the symbol stand out from the rest of the diagram. The entity can be identified by a lower-case letter in the upper left-hand corner for reference.

To avoid crossing data flow lines, the same entity can be drawn more than once on the same diagram; the two (or more) boxes per entity can be identified by an angled line in the bottom right-hand corner.

Where another entity is to be duplicated, the instances of it have two angled lines, and so on.

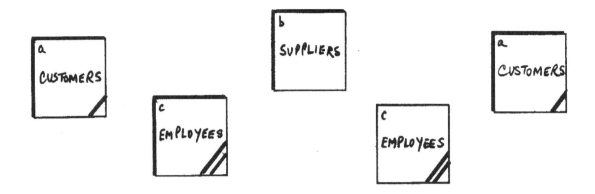

By designating some thing or some system as an external
entity, we are implicitly stating it is outside the boundary
of the system we are considering. As the analysis proceeds,
and we learn more about the user's objectives, we may take
some external entities and bring them into our system data
flow diagram, or alternatively, take some part of our system
function and remove it from consideration by designating it
all as an external entity with data flows to and from it.

DATA FLOW

This is symbolized by an arrow, preferably horizontal and/or
vertical, with an arrowhead showing the direction of flow.
For clarity, and especially in early drafts of the diagram,
a double-headed arrow may be used in place of two arrows,
where data flows are paired.

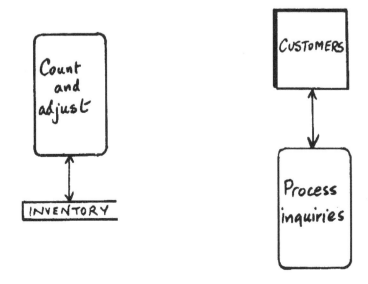

3.2 Dataflows and Contents

Each data flow is to be thought of as a pipe, down which parcels of data are sent. The data flow pipe may be referenced by giving the processes, entities, or data stores, at its head and tail, but each data flow should have a description of its contents written alongside it. A description should be chosen which is as meaningful as possible to the users who will be reviewing the data flow diagram, (consistent with being a logical description). In early versions, the data flow description should be written on the diagram in upper and lower case letters.

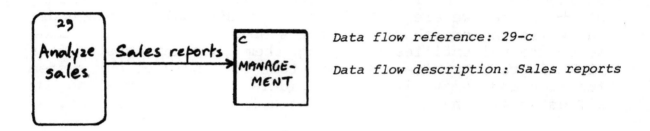

Data flow reference: 29-c

Data flow description: Sales reports

At a later stage of analysis, when the data dictionary contents have been defined, the description can be changed to all upper - case letters to show that it has been entered into the data dictionary. Frequently we find that several different "parcels" of data travel along the same data flow. For example, if we look up SALES-REPORTS in the data dictionary we may find its components listed as:

SALES-REPORTS-BY-DAY
SALES-TREND-ANALYSIS
SALESMAN-PERFORMANCE-ANALYSIS
SALES-BY-PRODUCT-ANALYSIS

Each of these components is in turn described in the data dictionary; each will contain a somewhat different assemblage of data elements.

Especially when drafting a data flow diagram, it is acceptable to leave out the description if it will be self-evident to the reviewer, but the creator of the diagram must be able to supply a description at all times.

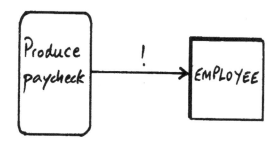

Occasionally it is difficult to find a description which adequately characterizes the contents of a data flow. For instance, customers may send in orders, payments, returns of damaged merchandise, inquiries, complaints, etc. It is unwieldy to draw:

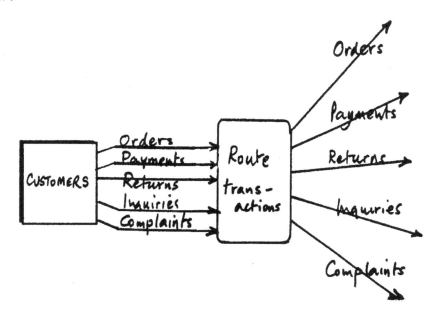

There are two ways out of such a situation. If the most important logical fact is that there is only a single data flow (perhaps to a sales office) and that the function "route transactions" is an important one, then the approach should be to lump the contents together under a necessarily vague term, such as "transactions from customers" or "management reports". The contents of this data flow can either be found in the data dictionary or by examining the output of the routing function.

41

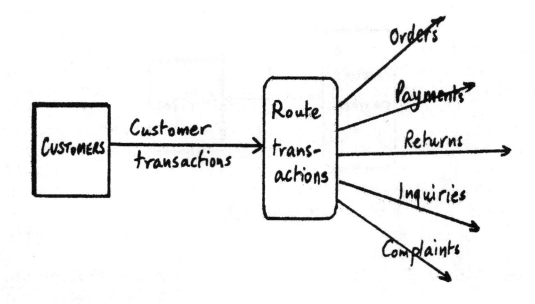

The second approach can be used where the routing funct-ion is trivial and each transaction gets processed in a dif-ferent way (and indeed consists of different data elements). In this case, a different arrow can be drawn for each different type of transaction, each going to a different process box:

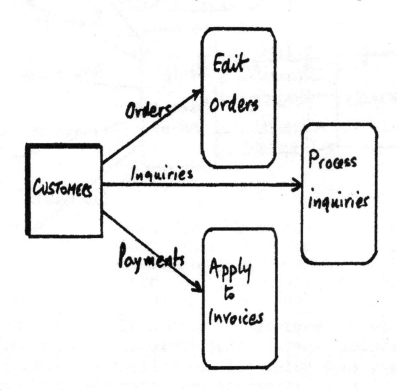

We need to describe the function of each process and, for easy reference, give each process a unique identifier, possibly tying it back to a physical system. Processes can be symbolized by an upright rectangle, with the corners rounded, optionally divided into three areas:

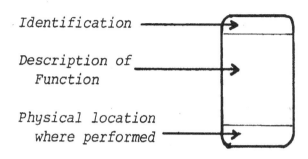

The *identification* can be a number, initially allocated approximately left to right across a data flow diagram, but having no meaning other than to identify the process. There is no point in assigning meaning to process numbers, since some processes will get split into two or more processes, (implying that new numbers have to be assigned) or several processes will get amalgamated into one (implying that numbers disappear) during the work of analysis. Once assigned, the process identification should not be changed, except for splitting or amalgamation, since it serves as a reference for the data flows and for the decomposition of the process to lower levels. For clarity, the fine lines dividing identification and description may be omitted, especially when the diagram is to be shown to users.

The *description of function* should be an imperative sentence, ideally consisting of an active verb (extract, compute, verify) followed by an object or object clause, the simpler the better, for example:

Extract – monthly sales
Enter – new customer details
Verify – customer is credit-worthy

If in doubt, it helps to think of the function description as though it were an "order to a dumb clerk". If the description would be unambiguous to a clerk, and if you can envisage the function being carried out in a simple clerical circumstance in 5 - 30 minutes, you probably have a good function description.

Generally speaking, when you find yourself using as verbs "process," "update," or "edit," it means that you probably do not understand much about that function yet, and that it will need further analysis.

"Create," "produce," "extract," "retrieve," "store," "compute," "calculate," "determine," "verify," are all active, unambiguous verbs. "Check" can be used but may lead to confusion with the noun in accounting or financial areas. "Sort" implies that a physical solution has been chosen, since sorting is merely a physical rearrangement of the sequence of records in a file, and has no *logical* value.

Note that these imperative sentences have no subject; as soon as a subject is introduced, (e.g., "Sales administrator extracts monthly sales") a physical commitment has been made as to how the function will be carried out. It may be helpful when studying an existing system, to note which department, or which program, carries out a function. Similarly, when the analysis is complete, and the physical design of the new system is underway, it is convenient to be able to note how the function will physically be done. This is the purpose of the optional lower part of the process box; to carry a *physical reference*, thus:

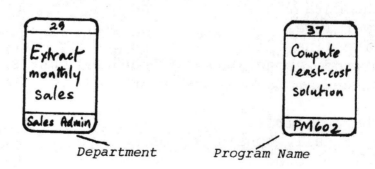

Department   Program Name

In this way, the logical function description and the physical implementation can be kept separate.

44

DATA STORE

Without making a physical commitment, we find during analysis that there are places where we need to define data as being stored between processes. Data stores can be symbolized by a pair of horizontal parallel lines, closed at one end, preferably just wide enough to hold the name, (¼" on an un-reduced diagram). Each store can be identified by a "D" and an arbitrary number in a box at the left - hand end, for easy reference.

D3 | ACCOUNTS RECEIVABLE

The name should be chosen to be most descriptive to the user.

To avoid complicating a data flow diagram with crossed lines, the same data store can be drawn more than once on the same diagram, identifying duplicate data stores by addition-al vertical lines at the left.

D1 | CUSTOMERS   D2 | EMPLOYEES   D1 | CUSTOMERS

When a process *stores* data, the data flow arrow is shown going *into* the data store, conversely, where a data store is *accessed in a read - only manner*, it is enough to show the group of data elements retrieved on the data flow coming out, thus:

    Storing Data   Accessing Data

45

3.3 Processes and Explosion

If it is necessary to specify the *search argument*, this may be shown on the opposite side of the data flow to the description; an arrowhead indicates that the search argument is passed to the data store from the process.

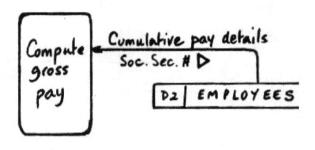

EXPLOSION CONVENTIONS

each process in the top-level data flow diagram for a system can be "exploded" to become a data flow diagram in its own right. Each process at the lower level will need to be related back to the high-level process. This can be done by giving the lower level process box an identification number which is a decimal of the high-level process box, i.e. 29 is decomposed into 29.1, 29.2, 29.3, etc., and, should it be necessary to go to a third level, 29.3 is decomposed into 29.3.1, 29.3.2, and so on.

The clearest representation of the explosion process is to draw lower level data flow diagrams within the boundary which represents the higher level process box. Obviously all data flows into and out of the higher level process box must enter and leave the boundary. Data flows which are shown for the first time at the lower level, such as error paths, can also leave the boundary. Where they do so, they can be high-lighted with an "X" at the exit point. Data stores are only shown within the boundary if they are created and accessed by this process, and by none other.

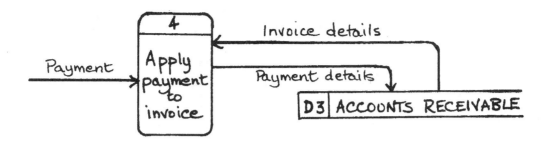

This "explosion" illustrates a number of graph ical points:

1.   Data stores which are "external" to the process being exploded can intrude on the boundary, if drawing them that way simplifies the diagram. D3-ACCOUNTS RECEIV-ABLE is really outside APPLY PAYMENT TO INVOICE, and has been drawn half-in half-out, for clarity. The three data flows, "D3-4.4 Invoice details," "D3-4.3 Invoice details," and "D3-4.9 Payment record," all cross the boundary.

2.   Data store D4/1, UNTRACED PAYMENTS, exists only for the internal purposes of this process, and so is shown inside. If it were accessed by any process not part of 4 APPLY PAYMENT TO INVOICE it would have to be shown as external (like D1 CUSTOMERS). We have used a convention, D4/1, to indicate the first internal data store in process 4. It has no necessary relationship to any data store called D4 in the parent diagram.

3.   External entities are not shown within the boundaries of explosions, even if, like BANK in this case, they may not be involved in any other process.

4.   Where it is inevitable that one data flow has to cross another, we use the "little hoop" convention,

as exemplified by "4.4-4.7 Invoice + payment details.'

5.   In the rare case when a data flow needs to cross a data store, as with "4.9-4.8 Payment details," it is also "hooped," as shown.

47

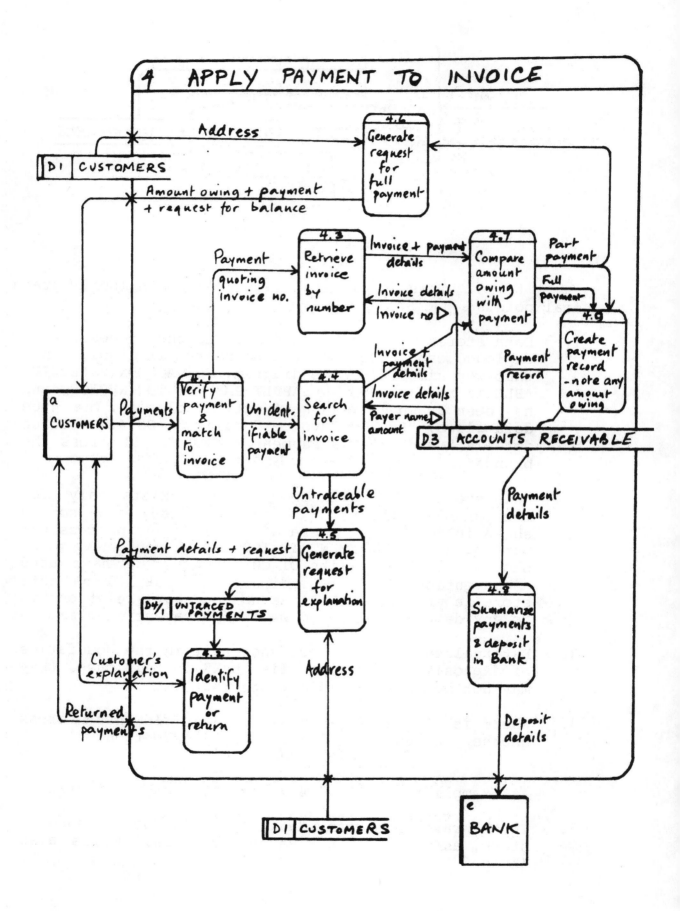

3.4 Guidelines for Drawing Dataflow Diagrams

In this section we summarize the steps involved in drawing up a data flow diagram for an existing or proposed system, before going on to develop an example in the next section.

1. Identify the external entities involved. As we said previously, this involves deciding on a preliminary system boundary. If in doubt, include within your system boundary the first "outer layer" of manual and automated systems with which you will have to interface. Remember that data flows are created when something happens in the outside world; a person decides to buy something, or an accident happens, or a truck arrives at the loading bay. If you can, get right back to the ultimate source of your data and draw the flow from there.

2. Identify the inputs and the outputs that you can expect and schedule in the normal course of business. As the list grows, try to discover logical groupings of inputs and outputs. Mark the inputs and outputs that are related solely to error and exception conditions.

3. Identify the inquiries and on-demand requests for information that could arise, involving pairs of data flows, in which one data flow specifies what is "given" to the system, and the second specifies what is "required" from the system.

4. Take a large sheet of paper (the back of used printer output is good), and starting on the left-hand side with the external entity that seems to you to be the prime source of inputs (e.g., Customers), draw the data flows that arise, processes that are logically necessary, and the data stores that you think will be required.

    Pay no attention to timing considerations except for natural logical precedence and logically necessary data stores. Draw a system that never started and will never stop. It's sometimes useful to follow a typical good input transaction all the way through the system and ask yourself, "What needs to happen to this transaction next?"

49

3.5 Order Processing and Distribution

Follow the notation rules set out in Section 3.1, but **don't** number processes until the final draft.

5. Draw the first draft freehand, and concentrate on getting everything down, except errors, exceptions, and decisions. If you find yourself drawing a diamond for a decision, slap your hand---decisions are made within low - level processes and do not appear on data flow diagrams.

6. Accept that you will need at least three drafts of the high-level data flow. Don't be concerned that the first draft looks like a hopeless tangle. It can be sorted out (see example in the next section).

7. When you have a first draft, check back with your list of inputs and outputs to ensure that you have included everything except those that deal with errors and exceptions. Note on the draft any normal inputs and outputs that you couldn't fit in. Remember that every data store which describes something outside in the real world has to be created and maintained.

8. Now produce a clearer second draft using a template for the symbols. You are aiming for a diagram with unique processes and the minimum number of crossing data flows. To minimize crossing:

    - first duplicate external entities, if needs be
    - next duplicate data stores, if needs be
    - then allow data flows to cross, if you can't see
        a layout that reduces crossing.

    Your second draft will look much clearer, but will probably still have some unnecessary crossings, and as you review it, you will see that the layout and relationship of process symbols could be improved.

    Check back to your list of inputs and outputs, and note on the second draft anything you still cannot fit in.

9. If you have a sympathetic user representative, or someone who knows the application, conduct a walkthrough of the second draft with them, explaining that it is only a draft, and noting any change resulting from the walkthrough.

The net figure shows a freehand sketch of the first few steps in order processing.

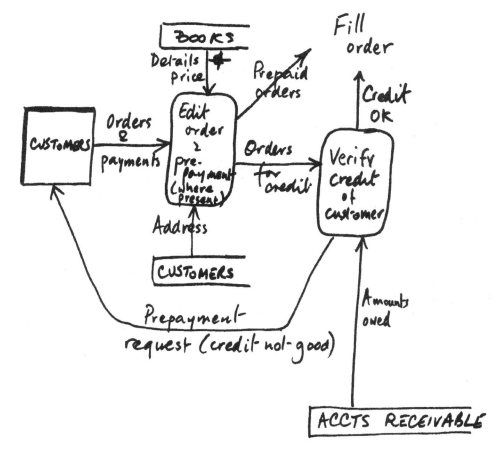

Partial First Draft

Our next task is to spell out what we mean by the note "Fill order."

Here we take orders and access the current inventory to see whether we can fill them or not. For those that we can fill, we generate a shipping note (which may be used in the warehouse to actually take the proper books out of stock) and an invoice (which will need to be marked "Paid" in the case where we have already received the payment with the order). The sketch is becoming a little complex, but we can see how the system is growing. We continue in this way, and end up with a first draft of the whole system.

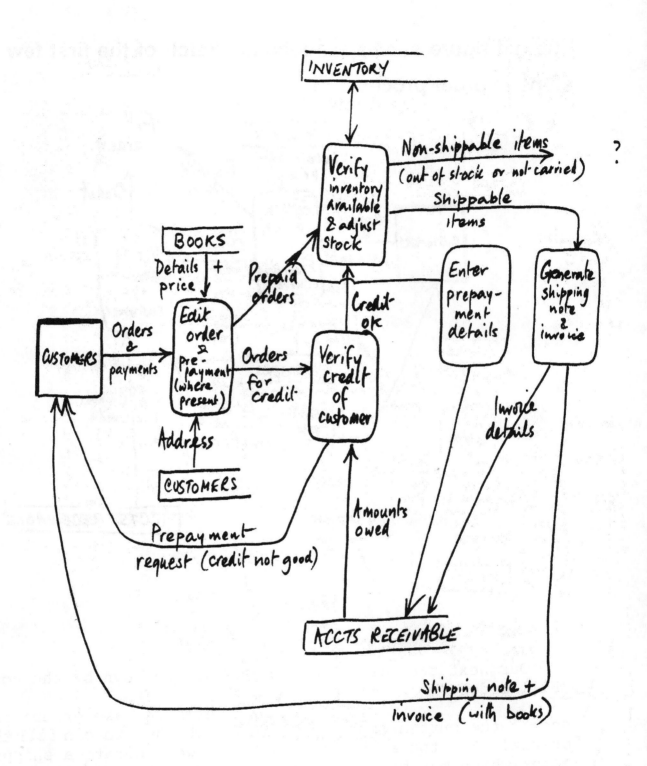

Extended First Draft

52

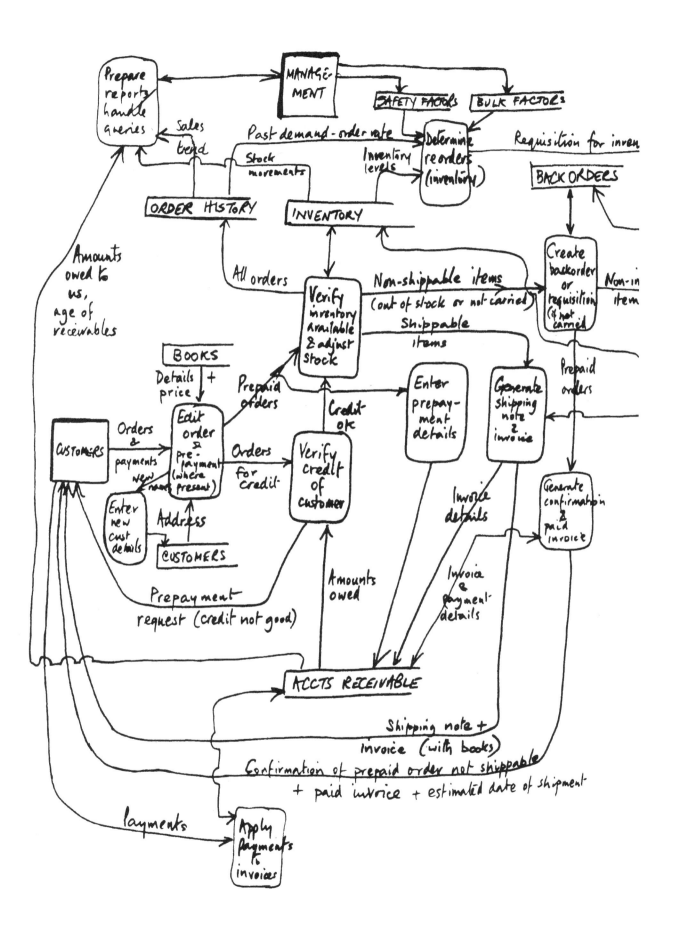

ANDREAS SOFRONIOU

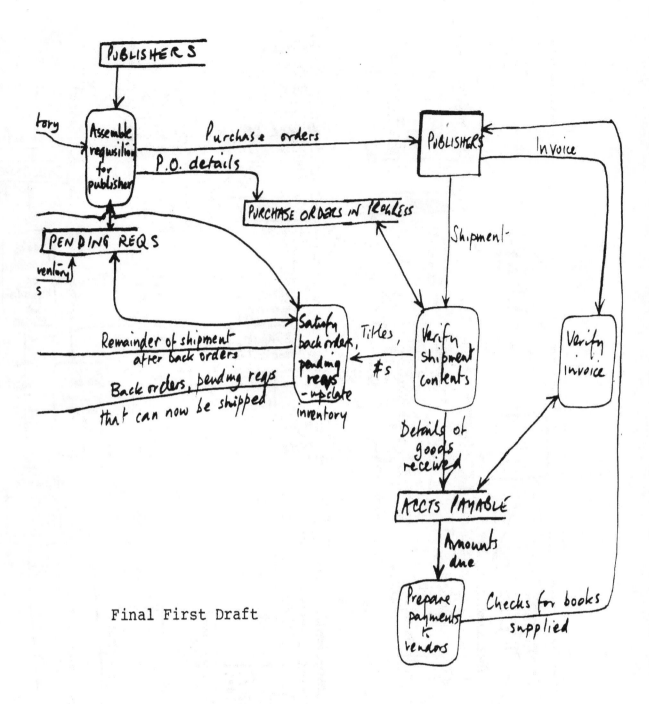

Final First Draft

As you can see, this first draft can get quite cluttered and tangled; it's only as you identify data flows and processes that you can see how they fit together, so it is almost impossible to get a good layout first time through. At least we now have all the major features of the system on one piece of paper. The next step is to redraw the first draft using a template.

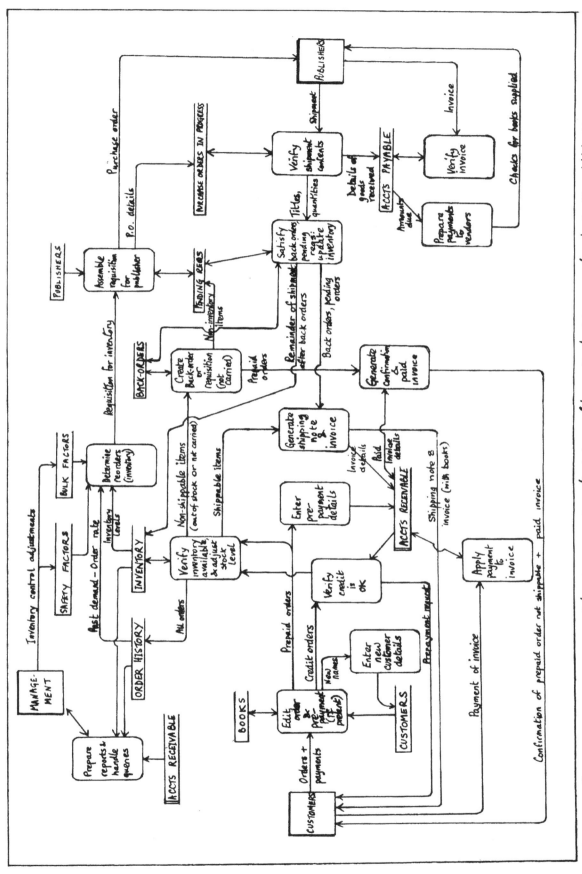

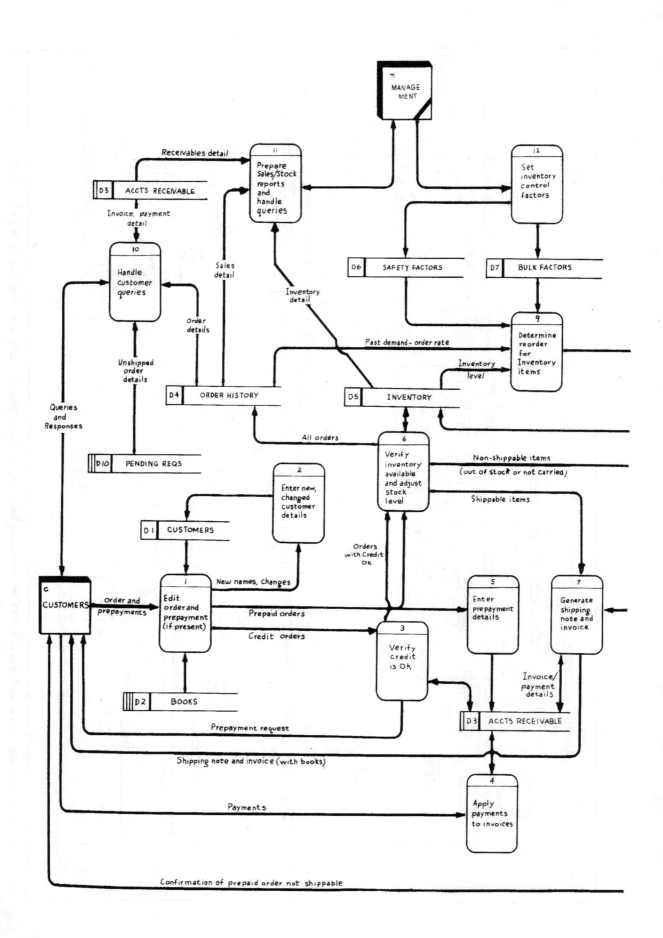

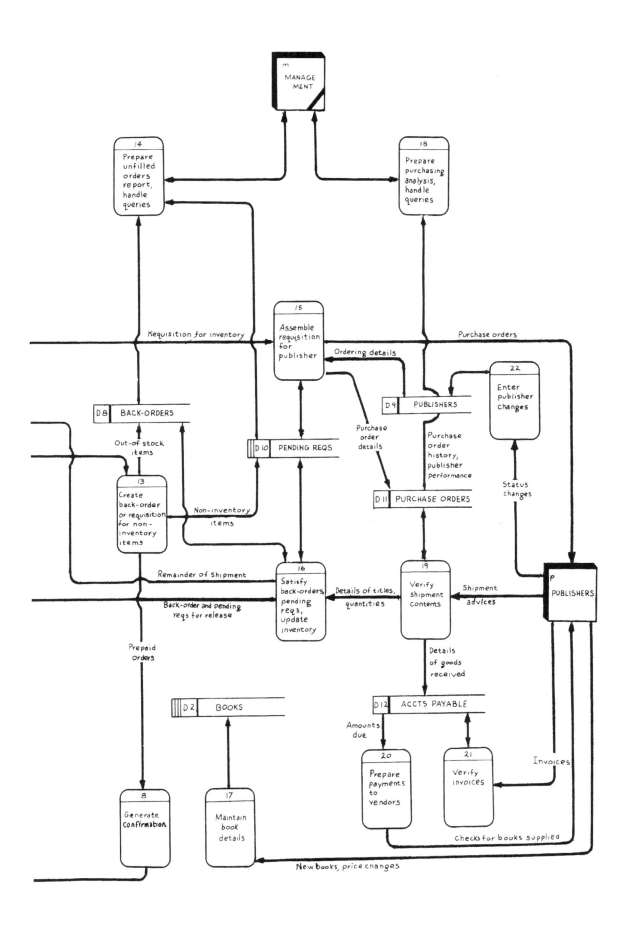

57

3.6   MATERIALS FLOW AND DATA FLOW

At several points when describing the system we have just char-
ted, we commented that we were tempted to describe a materials
flow instead of, as is correct, the associated data flow. It
is important to keep these two concepts separate, especially
in manufacturing and distribution industries, where much of
the business is concerned with moving material around. Even
in banking, the business of which might be thought to be as
near as we can get to pure data, there are serious problems
relating to the physical movement of large numbers of checks
and other vouchers.

Consequently, we need a way of charting materials flow,
when required, and tying the materials flow diagram to the
data flow diagram. Materials flow is by its very nature
physical, but we would like, as far as possible, to describe
the operations performed on the materials in logical terms.

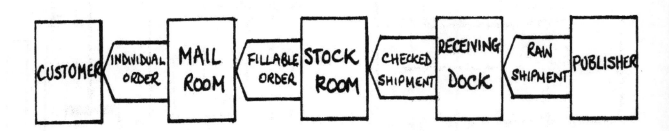

but will need some way of describing the logical function
which transforms the material at each point, and indicating
the associated data flows.

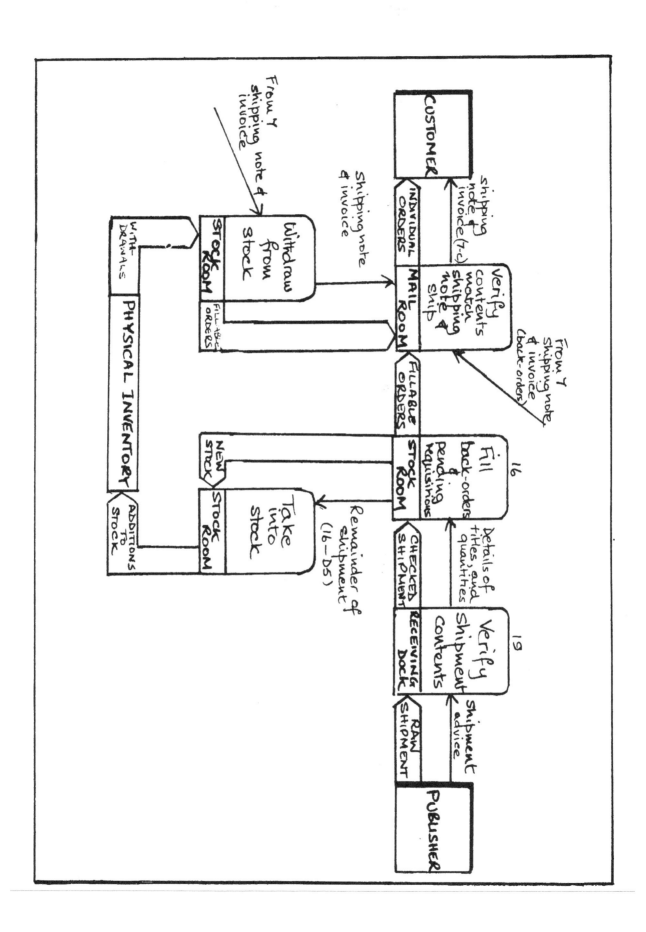

4. BUILDING AND USING A DATA DICTIONARY

4.1 Problem of Describing Data

In the good old unit-record days, the terms used to describe data were simple. Card was divided into fields; the card itself was a record, and a number of records constituted a file.

It was not quite as simple as that; a date field in the form DDMMYY could be thought of as composed of three subfields, so already the data description hierarchy existed at four levels:

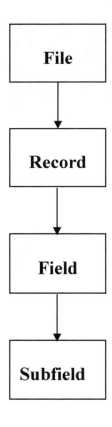

4.2 Data Dictionary Contents

Here we may want to look at the attributes of dataflows, datastores, processes, external entities and other things encountered in analysis. This will give us a background for assessing any data dictionary system, or for planning our own.

- **Data Element:** the minimum information needed to establish a data element is the 'name' and a 'description'.

- **Data Structures:** these are built up out of the data elements and other data structures.

- **Dataflows:** this can be the expression of the contents of a dataflow.

- **Datastores:** since a datastore is a data structure at rest we describe the contents of each datastore in terms of the data structures, which we will find in it.

- **Processes:** the logic of processes can be documented with several tools, such as; decision trees, decision tables, and structured English.

- **External Entities:** the description of these can be associated with dataflows, person or group of people, or where the external entity is another system.

In defining a process in the data dictionary, the inputs and outputs are specified. The reader may note that there are a number of pitfalls in expressing logic in narrative English.

4.3 Importance of Third Normal Form (3NF)

3NF is the simplest possible representation of data that we can get. It represents a kind of 'inspired common sense', in that often we can expand the contents of data stores down into data structures in 3NF.

The basic simplicity of data in 3NF makes it much more flexible and easy to change, compared to other methods of organising a physical database.

So, as analysts, we can use 3NF as to kill three birds with one stone:

- We can use 3NF relations as the basic building blocks of the datastores.
- As the standard medium for communicating the contents of datastores to the physical designer.
- We can show the logical contents of datastores to interested users in the familiar form of tables.

To see how the techniques of normalisation work out in practice, please review the following hand drawn draft diagram, which represents the 'Order Entry' subsystem of the Company.

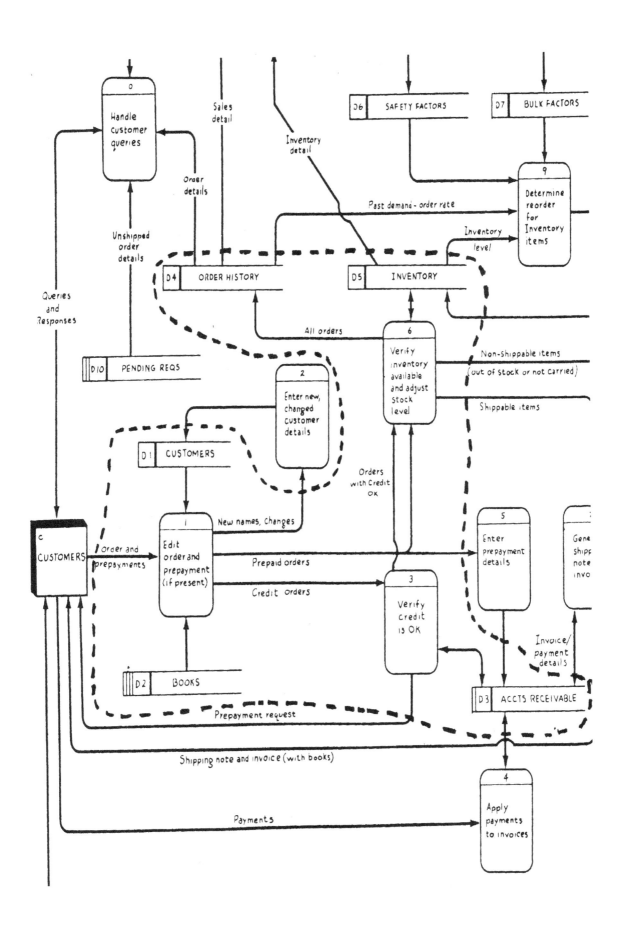

As you can see,we are concerned with
four logical data stores:

>   D1: CUSTOMERS
>   D2: *BOOKS*
>   D3: ACCOUNTS RECEIVABLE
>   D5: INVENTORY

We will assume for the purposes of this example that the raw
contents of each of these data stores have been defined in
the data dictionary, based on an examination of the data
flows into and out of each data store,
"What comes out must go in." Let us take each
data store in turn, and normalize it.

NORMALIZATION OF THE "CUSTOMERS" DATA STORE

Suppose the data dictionary entry for CUSTOMERS specifies its
structure thus:

>   D1: CUSTOMERS
>
>   ORGANIZATION-NAME
>
>   ORGANIZATION-ADDRESS*(1-)
>   STREET-BOX
>   CITY-COUNTY
>   STATE-ZIP
>
>   PHONE
>   AREA-CODE
>   EXCHANGE
>   NUMBER
>
>   CONTACT*(1-)
>   CONTACT-NAME
>   [JOB-TITLE]
>   [PHONE-EXTENSION]

From this data structure we see that we can expect any
organization to have one or more locations.

64

5. STRUCTURED METHODOLOGY

5.1 Initial Study

The questions that should be answered by an initial study are:

- What is wrong with the current situation?
- What improvement is possible?
- Who will be affected by the new system?

By the end of the initial study, the analyst should be reasonably confident about the magnitude of the benefits that could result from a new system.

5.2 Detailed Study

The outcome of the initial study will be reviewed by the appropriate level of management and a detailed study may be authorised. T this level, the study should include:

- The definition in more detail of who of the users of a new system would be.
- Building a logical model of the current system.
- Refining the estimates.

The estimates of the probable replacement system should incorporate; costs, timescales, and the definition of possible alternatives.

5.3 Defining a 'Menu' of Alternatives

The activities involved in the development of the 'menu' include:

- Deriving objectives or the new system from the limitations of the current system.
- Developing a logical model of the new system.
- Producing tentative alternative physical designs.

5.4 Using the 'Menu' to get Commitment from Users

Once the 'Menu' has been formulated, it must be presented to the manager/s to make the investment decision. In the meantime, the analyst should make a presentation covering the following points:

- The current system (if one exists).
- The limitations of the current system or situation.
- The logical model of the new system.
- Each of the alternative systems that make up the menu.
- A request for direction as to which of the alternatives represents the best cost-effective trade-off in the users' eyes.

5.5 Refining the Physical Design of the New System

Once a commitment has been made by the user decision makers, the analyst and the designer should work together to translate the logical model and the tentative physical design, into a firm physical design.

This process involves four overlapping activities:

- Refining the logical model.

- Designing the physical new database.

- Deriving the hierarchy of modular functions that will be programmed.

- Defining the new clerical tasks that will interface with new system.

5.6 Contents for Analysis

Since this book is on analysis, and not primarily on design, nor implementation, we shall not carry the structure and the following phases in subsequent development of the system:

- Drawing up an implementation plan.

- The concurrent development of the application programs.

- The conversion and loading of the database.

- The testing and acceptance of each part of the system.

The analyst frequently acts as an agent for the users in these later phases.

Further on, the logical model should be kept up to date through design and implementation, especially the dataflow diagram. It will serve as prime tool for planning enhancements especially those which involve new functions.

6. INTRODUCING STRUCTURED SYSTEMS

In this final chapter we consider the steps that need to be taken to introduce the tools and techniques discussed in this book into system development organisation, and then consider the benefits that may reasonably be expected together with the problems that people have experienced.

6.1 Implementation of Structured Systems Analysis

In the past we have tended to assume that a well managed development project went in a 'straight line' from feasibility study through analysis through design into testing, acceptance, operation and training.

The following figure shows this 'ideal' of project progress diagrammatically.

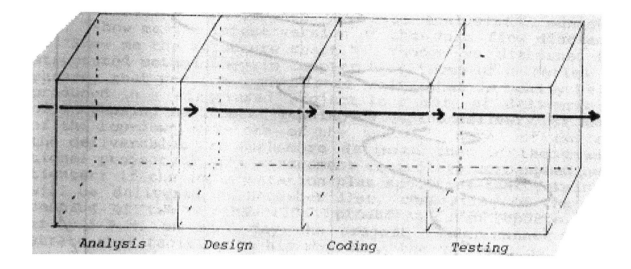

Clean and manageable as the straight line may be, it does not appear to correspond to the realities of system development.

Even a well managed project, staffed by competent people, needs to proceed iteratively, doing some analysis, then more design, then coding the first version, perhaps, then more design and so on.

The path of such a project can be pictured as a 'spiral', as shown in the next figure.

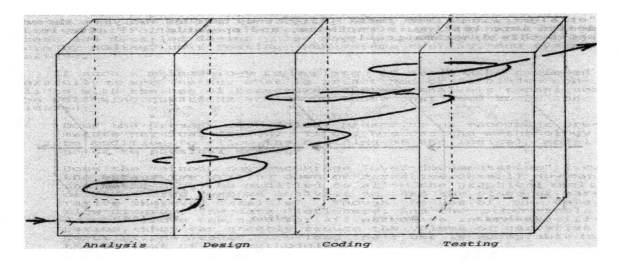

The reality of 'spiralling' projects is the right approach, which reflects the reality of the difficult problems we face in developing a new system, the way the users want it; as well as top-down development, structured analysis and designing.

6.2 Inclusive Activities in Implementation

Other inclusive activities, or steps in the implementation of the structured approach are:

•   Reviewing the ground rules for conducting projects.

•   Establishing standards and procedures for the use of the data dictionary and other software.

•   Training analysts and participating users in the use of the tools and techniques.

•   Orienting users to the new approach.

7. BENEFITS AND PROBLEMS

7.1 Benefits

With structured coding or top-down development, it is possible to quantify some of the benefits that result; improved productivity in lines of codes per day, more manageable use of the test time, and so on.

With structured design, the benefits are just as real, which can be itemised here:

• Users get a much more vivid idea of the proposed system.

• Presenting the system in terms of logical dataflow shows up misunderstanding and contentious issues.

• The interfaces between the new system and existing operations are shown very clearly by the dataflow diagrams.

• The use of the logical model does away with a certain amount of duplication of effort.

• The use of the data dictionary to hold project glossary items saves time by quickly resolving those cases where people call the same things by different names.

71

7.2 Potential Problems

The problems of the new analytical tools are not free, of course; there are some costs and potential problems associated with their introductions. Partly there are the problems associated with the change; partly they are results of the greater formality and discipline of the logical tools.

These may include:

- Orientation of the users and training of analysts is required.

- The effort, formality and degree of detail required is often resisted.

- There has been uneasiness on the part of programmers that getting detailed specifications of logic in Structured English will 'take all the fun out of programming and make them more of coders'.

- Lastly, a question arises in some organisations after their first positive experience with structured systems analysis.

8. GLOSSARY

In this final part of the book, the most common of terms are included, in the hope that these will enable the reader and the users to familiarise themselves with the vocabulary used in discussing computing in general.

Although some of the terminology is not used in the writing of this book, it is hoped that the reader will find the additional explanation of each term helpful in the understanding of the phrases used in the analysis and designing of a system.

Thus comprehending the reality of what can be involved.

The jargon selected for this purpose is listed below:

ALIAS

a name or symbol which stands for something, and is not its proper name.

ARGUMENT

a value which is used as the input to some process, often passed through a module-module interface.

ATTRIBUTE

a data element which holds information about an entity.

CANDIDATE-KEY

an attribute or group of attributes, whose values uniquely identify every tuple in a relation, and for which none of the attributes can be removed without destroying the unique identification.

COINCIDENTAL COHESION

used to describe a module which has no meaningful relationship between its components (other than that they happen to be in the same module). The weakest module strength.

COMMUNICATIONAL COHESION

used to describe a module in which all the components operate on the same data structure. A good, but not ideal module strength.

CONTENT COUPLING

a severe form of coupling, in which one module makes a direct reference to the contents of another module.

CONTINUOUS DATA ELEMENT

one which can take so many values within its range that it is not practical to enumerate them, e.g., a sum of money.

CONTROL COUPLING

a form of coupling in which one module passes one or more flags or switches to another, as part of invocation or returning control.

DATA ADMINISTRATOR (DATA BASE ADMINISTRATOR)

a person (or group) responsible for the control and integrity of a set of files (data bases).

DATA AGGREGATE

a named collection of data items (data elements) within a record.

See also: GROUP

DATA BASE

"a collection of interrelated data stored together with controlled redundancy to serve one or more applications; the data are stored so that they are independent of programs which use the data; a common and controlled approach is used in adding new data and in modifying and in retrieving existing data within a data base."

James Martin

DATA DICTIONARY

a data store that describes the nature of each piece of data used in a system; often including process descriptions, glossary entries, and other items.

DATA DIRECTORY

a data store, usually machine-readable, that tells where each piece of data is stored in a system.

DATA ELEMENT (DATA ITEM, FIELD)

the smallest unit of data that is meaningful for the purpose at hand.

DATA FLOW DIAGRAM (DFD)

a picture of the flows of data through a system of any kind, showing the external entities which are sources or destinations of data, the processes which transform data, and the places where the data is stored.

DATA IMMEDIATE-ACCESS DIAGRAM (DIAD)

a picture of the immediate access paths into a data stor showing what the users require to retrieve from the data store without searching or sorting it.

DATA ITEM

See DATA ELEMENT.

DATA STORE

any place in a system where data is stored between trans actions or between executions of the system (includes files--manual and machine readable, data bases, and tables).

DATA STRUCTURE

one or more data elements in a particular relationship, usually used to describe some entity.

DECISION TABLE

a tabular chart showing the logic relating various combinations of conditions to a set of actions. Usually all possible combinations of conditions are dealt with in the table.

DECISION TREE

a branching chart showing the actions that follow from various combinations of conditions.

DEGREE (OF NORMALIZED RELATION)

the number of domains making up the relation. (If there are 7 domains, the relation is 7-ary or of degree 7).

DESIGN

The (iterative) process of taking a logical model of a system, together with a strongly-stated set of objectives for that system, and producing the specification of a physical system that will meet those objectives.

DFD

See DATA FLOW DIAGRAM.

DIAD

See DATA IMMEDIATE ACCESS DIAGRAM

DISCRETE DATA ELEMENT

one which takes up only a limited number of values, each of which usually has a meaning.

See also: CONTINUOUS DATA ELEMENT.

DOMAIN

the set of all values of a data element that is part of a relation. Effectively equivalent to a field, or data element.

EE

See EXTERNAL ENTITY.

ENTITY

1. external entity: a source or destination of data on a data flow diagram

2. something about which information is stored in a data store e.g., customer, employees

---

77

EXTERNAL COUPLING

a severe form of intermodule coupling in which one module refers to elements inside another module, and such elements have been declared to be accessible to other modules.

EXTERNAL ENTITY (EE)

See ENTITY.

FACTORED

a function or logical module is factored when it is decomposed into subfunctions or submodules.

FIRST NORMAL FORM (1NF)

a relation without repeating groups (a normalized relation), but not meeting the stiffer tests for second or third normal form.

FUNCTIONAL

1. functional cohesion: used to describe a module all of whose components contribute towards the performance of a single function.

2. functional dependence: a data element A is functionally dependent on another data element B, if given the value of B, the corresponding value of A is determined.

GROUP (ITEM)

a data structure composed of a small number of data elements, with a name, referred to as a whole.

See also: DATA AGGREGATE.

HIPO (HIERARCHICAL INPUT PROCESS OUTPUT)

a graphical technique similar to the structure chart showing a logical model of a modular hierarchy. A HIPO overview diagram shows the hierarchy of modules: details of each module's input processing and output are shown on a separate detail diagram, one per module.

IMMEDIATE ACCESS

retrieval of a piece of data from a data store faster than it is possible to read through the whole data store searching for the piece of data, or to sort the data store.

INDEX

a data store that, as part of a retrieval process, takes information about the value(s) of some attribute(s) and returns with information that enables the record(s) with those attributes to be retrieved quickly.

INVERTED FILE

one in which multiple indexes to the data are provided; the data may itself be contained within the indexes.

IRACIS

acronym for Increased Revenue, Avoidable Costs, Improved Service.

KEY

a data element (or group of data elements) used to find or identify a record (tuple).

LEXICAL

to do with the order in which program statements are written. Module A is lexically included within module B if A's statements come within B's statements on the source listing.

LOGICAL

1. non-physical (of an entity, statement, or chart): capable of being implemented in more than one way, expressing the underlying nature of the system referred to.

2. logical cohesion: used to describe a module which carries out a number of similar, but slightly different functions--a poor module strength.

79

MODULE

1. a logical module: a function or set of functions referred to by name.

2. a physical module: a contiguous sequence of program statements, bounded by a boundary element, referred to by name.

NORMALIZED (RELATION)

a relation (file), without repeating groups, such that the values of the data elements (domains) could be represented as a two-dimensional table.

ON-LINE

connected directly to the computer so that input, output, data access, and computation can take place without further human intervention.

PATHOLOGICAL (CONNECTION)

a severe form of coupling between modules where one module refers to something inside another module.

See also: CONTENT COUPLING

PERSONNEL SUBSYSTEM

the data flows and processes, within a total information system, that are carried out by people: the documentation and training needed to establish such a subsystem.

PHYSICAL

to do with the particular way data or logic is represented or implemented at a particular time. A physical statement cannot be assigned more than one real-world implementation.

See also: LOGICAL.

PRIMARY KEY

a key which uniquely identifies a record (tuple).

PROCEDURAL COHESION

used to describe a module whose components make up two or more blocks of a flowchart. Not as good as communicational or functional cohesion.

PROCESS (TRANSFORM, TRANSFORMATION)

a set of operations transforming data, logically or physically, according to some process logic.

PSEUDOCODE

a tool for specifying program logic in English-like readable form, without conforming to the syntactical rules of any particular programming language.

RELATION

a file represented in normalized form, as a two-dimensional table of data elements.

RELATIONAL DATA BASE

a data base constructed out of normalized relations only

SCOPE-OF-CONTROL (OF A MODULE)

all of the modules which are invoked by a module; and all those invoked by the lower levels, and so on. The "department" of which the module is "boss."

SCOPE-OF-EFFECT (OF A DECISION)

all those modules whose execution or invocation depends upon the outcome of the decision.

SEARCH ARGUMENT

the attribute value(s) which are used to retrieve some data from a data store, whether through an index, or by a search.

See also: ARGUMENT.

SECOND NORMAL FORM (2NF)

a normalized relation in which all of the non-key domains are fully functionally dependent on the primary key.

SECONDARY INDEX

an index to a data store based on some attribute other than the primary key.

SEGMENT

a group of (one or more) data elements; the unit of data accessed by IMS software.

Compare GROUP, DATA AGGREGATE.

SIDE EFFECT

the lowering of a module's cohesion due to its doing some subfunctions which are "on the side," not part of the main function of the module.

SPAN OF CONTROL

the number of modules directly invoked by another module. This should not be very high (except in the case of a dispatcher module) or very low.

STRUCTURE CHART

a logical model of a modular hierarchy, showing invocation, intermodular communication (data and control), and the location of major loops and decisions. See Figure 9.32.

STRUCTURED DESIGN

a set of guidelines for producing a hierarchy of logical modules which represents a highly changeable system.

See also: DESIGN

82

STRUCTURED ENGLISH

a tool for representing policies and procedures in a precise form of English, using the logical structures of Structured Coding.

See also: PSEUDOCODE.

STRUCTURED PROGRAMMING (CODING)

the construction of programs using a small number of logical constructs, each one-entry, one-exit, in a nested hierarchy.

THIRD NORMAL FORM (3NF)

a normalized relation in which all of the non-key domains are fully functionally dependent on the primary key <u>and</u> all the non-key domains are mutually independent.

TIGHT ENGLISH

a tool for representing policies and procedures with the least possible ambiguity.

See also: STRUCTURED ENGLISH.

TSO

Time Sharing Option: a feature of IBM software which allows the entering and editing of programs and text through on-line terminals.

TOP-DOWN DEVELOPMENT

a development strategy whereby the executive control modules of a system are coded and tested first, to form a "skeleton" version of the system, and when the system interfaces have been proven to work, the lower level modules are coded and tested.

TUPLE

a specific set of values for the domains making up a relation. The "relational" term for a record.

See also: SEGMENT

VOLATILITY

a measure of the rate at which a file's contents change, especially in terms of addition of new records.

INDEX

BIBLIOGRAPHY

All books publications mentioned in this bibliography are written by Andreas Sofroniou

1. I.T. RISK MANAGEMENT, ISBN: 978-1-4467-5653-9
2. SYSTEMS ENGINEERING, ISBN: 978-1-4477-7553-9
3. BUSINESS INFORMATION SYSTEMS, CONCEPTS AND EXAMPLES, ISBN: 978-1-4092-7338-7
4. A GUIDE TO INFORMATION TECHNOLOGY, ISBN: 978-1-4092-7608-1
5. CHANGE MANAGEMENT IN I.T., ISBN: 978-1-4092-7712-5
6. FRONT-END DESIGN AND DEVELOPMENT FOR SYSTEMS APPLICATIONS, ISBN: 978-1-4092-7588-6
7. I.T RISK MANAGEMENT, ISBN: 978-1-4092-7488-9
8. THE SIMPLIFIED PROCEDURES FOR I.T. PROJECTS DEVELOPMENT, ISBN: 978-1-4092-7562-6
9. THE SIGMA METHODOLOGY FOR RISK MANAGEMENT IN SYSTEMS DEVELOPMENT, ISBN: 978-1-4092-7690-6
10. TRADING ON THE INTERNET IN THE YEAR 2000 AND BEYOND, ISBN: 978-1-4092- 7577
11. STRUCTURED SYSTEMS METHODOLOGY, ISBN: 978-1-4477-6610-0
12. INFORMATION TECHNOLOGY LOGICAL ANALYSIS, ISBN: 978-1-4717-1688-1
13. I.T. RISKS LOGICAL ANALYSIS, ISBN: 978-1-4717-1957-8
14. I.T. CHANGES LOGICAL ANALYSIS, ISBN: 978-1-4717-2288-2
15. LOGICAL ANALYSIS OF SYSTEMS, RISKS , CHANGES, ISBN: 978-1-4717-2294-3
16. COMPUTING, A PRÉCIS ON SYSTEMS, SOFTWARE AND HARDWARE, ISBN: 978-1-2910-5102-5
17. MANAGE THAT I.T. PROJECT, ISBN: 978-1-4717-5304-6
18. CHANGE MANAGEMENT, ISBN: 978-1-4457-6114-5
19. MANAGEMENT OF I.T. CHANGES, RISKS, WORKSHOPS, EPISTEMOLOGY, ISBN: 978-1-84753-147-6
20. THE MANAGEMENT OF COMMERCIAL COMPUTING, ISBN: 978-1-

4092-7550-3

21. PROGRAMME MANAGEMENT WORKSHOP, ISBN: 978-1-4092-7583-1

22. THE PHILOSOPHICAL CONCEPTS OF MANAGEMENT THROUGH THE AGES, ISBN: 978-1-4092- 7554-1

23. THE MANAGEMENT OF PROJECTS, SYSTEMS, INTERNET, AND RISKS, ISBN: 978-1-4092- 7464-3

24. HOW TO CONSTRUCT YOUR RESUMÊ, ISBN: 978-1-4092-7383-7

25. DEFINE THAT SYSTEM, ISBN: 978-1-291-15094-0

26. INFORMATION TECHNOLOGY WORKSHOP, ISBN: 978-1-291-16440-4

27. CHANGE MANAGEMENT IN SYSTEMS, ISBN: 978-1-4457-1099-0

28. SYSTEMS MANAGEMENT, ISBN: 978-1-4710-4907-1

29. TECHNOLOGY, A STUDY OF MECHANICAL ARTS AND APPLIED SCIENCES, ISBN: 978-1-291-58550-6

30. EXPERT SYSTEMS, KNOWLEDGE ENGINEERING FOR HUMAN REPLICATION, ISBN: 978-1-291- 59509-3

31. ARTIIFICIAL INTELLIGENCE AND INFORMATION TECHNOLOGY, ISBN: 978-1-291- 60445-0

32. PROJECT MANAGEMENT PROCEDURES FOR SYSTEMS DEVELOPMENT, ISBN: 978-0-952-72531-2

33. SURFING THE INTERNET, THEN, NOW, LATER. ISBN: 978-1--291-77653-9

Author's Biography

Andreas Sofroniou is a Business Director and an Information Technology Executive with U.K., U.S.A., and international organisations, an Expert on Computing for the European Union, a Principal Adviser to British Government Departments, a retired U.K. London Harley Street Consultant Psychotherapist, a Life Fellow of the Institute of Directors and a published author.

As an author, Andreas Sofroniou's ninety books were published by *PulishAmerica*, *Nielsen*, *Whitaker*, *PsySys,* & *lulu.com/sofroniou*. The titles include: *Social Sciences, Medical Sciences, Psychotherapy, Psychoanalysis, Psychology, Sociology, Philology, Philosophy, Epistemology, Politics, History, Management, Technology, Information Technology, Expert Systems, Artificial Intelligence, Fiction, and Poetry.*

www.ingramcontent.com/pod-product-compliance
Lightning Source LLC
Chambersburg PA
CBHW081227050326
40689CB00016B/3701